Simple Pleasures

50 popular recipes from PlainChicken.com

STEPHANIE PARKER

ISBN: 1479360635
ISBN-13: 978-1479360635

CONTENTS

Breakfast

Maple Sausage and Waffle Casserole

8 frozen Eggo homestyle waffles, cubed
16 ounces maple breakfast sausage, crumbled
1 cup shredded cheddar cheese
6 large eggs
1-1/4 cups whole or low-fat milk
1/4 cup maple syrup

Cook the sausage in a nonstick skillet over medium heat, breaking it apart with a wooden spoon, until well browned, 8 to 10 minutes. Drain fat.

Grease an 8-inch square baking dish. Add half of the cubed waffles in a single layer. Top with half of the sausage and 1/2 cup of the cheese. Layer the remaining waffles and sausage and 1/2 cup more cheese. Whisk together the eggs, milk, and maple syrup, in a medium bowl until combined. Pour the egg mixture evenly over the casserole.

Wrap the baking dish with plastic wrap and place refrigerate for at least 1 hour, or up to 1 day.

Bake at 325 degrees 45 to 50 minutes.
Serves 6

Easy Biscuit Waffles

1 can Grands Jr. Golden Layers biscuits
cooking spray
butter
syrup

Spray waffle maker with cooking spray. Heat waffle maker.

Separate dough into 10 biscuits. Place up to 4 biscuits at a time on waffle maker. Close lid of waffle maker; cook 1 to 2 minutes or until light golden brown. Serve immediately with butter and syrup.

Serves 5

Baked Blueberry Pancakes

3/4 cup milk
2 Tbsp melted butter, slightly cooled
1 large egg
1/2 tsp vanilla
1 Tbsp sugar
1 cup flour
2 tsp baking powder
1/4 tsp salt
1 cup blueberries

Preheat oven to 350.

Lightly grease an 8×8 baking dish. In a large mixing bowl, whisk together milk, butter, egg, and vanilla. Add sugar, flour, baking powder and salt. Carefully stir in blueberries. Pour batter into pan.

Bake for 20-25 minutes. Serve with butter and maple syrup.

Serves 4

McMuffin Casserole

4 English muffins, split (Bays)
6 oz Canadian bacon
1 cup cheddar cheese
4 eggs
1 1/4 cup milk
salt
pepper

Grease an 8-inch square baking dish. Cube English muffins and chop Canadian bacon. Add half of the cubed English muffins in a single layer. Top with half of the Canadian bacon and 1/2 cup of the cheese.

Layer the remaining English muffins and Canadian bacon and 1/2 cup more cheese.

Whisk together the eggs, milk, salt, and pepper in a medium bowl until combined. Pour the egg mixture evenly over the casserole. Wrap the baking dish with plastic wrap and place refrigerate for at least 1 hour, or up to 1 day.

Bake at 325 degrees 45 to 50 minutes. Allow to cool for 10 minutes and serve with syrup, if desired.
Serves 4

Cinnamon Roll Pulls

Cinnamon Roll Pulls

1 unsliced round loaf sourdough bread

1/2 cup butter, softened
1/4 cup powdered sugar
1/4 cup honey
1 tsp pure vanilla extract

1 cup sugar
1 1/4 tsp cinnamon

1 cup powdered sugar
1-2 Tbsp milk

Preheat oven to 350 degrees.

To make Vanilla Honey Butter: Whip butter and 1/4 cup powdered sugar together until smooth; stir in honey and vanilla. Set aside. (You can use regular butter if desired)

Cut the bread lengthwise into 1/2" slices, without cutting through the bottom crust. Spread vanilla honey butter in between slices. Rotate the bread 90 degrees and slice the bread again into 1/2" pieces, without cutting through the bottom crust. Spread more vanilla honey butter in between new cuts. This doesn't need to be perfect - just make sure there is lots of butter in between all the cuts. Combine sugar and cinnamon. Generously sprinkle in between all cuts. (You may have extra butter and cinnamon sugar. It will just depend on how large your bread loaf is.)

Wrap in foil; place on a baking sheet. Bake at 350 degrees for 25-30 minutes, until bread is warm. Unwrap cinnamon bread and place on serving platter. Combine powdered sugar and milk - adding milk until you get the consistency desired. Drizzle icing over bread and serve immediately.

Cracked Out Quiche

1 9-inch deep dish pie crust
3 oz bacon pieces
1 cup shredded cheddar cheese
3 eggs
1/4 cup milk (I used 1%)
1/4 cup heavy cream
1/2 cup light Ranch dressing

Preheat oven to 375.

Place bacon in bottom of pie crust. Top with cheese. Whisk together eggs, milk, and Ranch dressing. Pour over bacon and cheese. Bake for 40-50 minutes, until center is sct and the quiche is lightly browned. Allow to cool for at least 5 minutes before serving.

Southwestern Quichiladas

1 lb sausage, cooked and crumbled
1 can Rotel tomatoes, drained
2 1/2 cups shredded cheddar cheese, divided
6 eggs
2 cups half and half
10 flour tortillas

Assemble this casserole the night before and bake it in the morning.
Spray a 9x13-inch pan with cooking spray. Set aside.
Mix together sausage, Rotel tomatoes and 2 cups of cheddar cheese. Divide meat and cheese mixture between tortillas. Roll up each tortilla and place seam side down in baking dish.

Whisk together half and half and eggs. Pour over tortillas. Cover and let sit overnight.

When ready to bake, preheat oven to 350. Bake covered for 30-40 minutes. Remove foil and sprinkle remaining 1/2 cup of cheese over enchiladas.
Bake for 5-10 more minutes, until cheese is melted.
Top with salsa if desired.

Serves 5

English Muffin French Toast

1 cup Egg Beaters
1 cup milk (I use 1%)
1 tsp vanilla
6 english muffins - split

Mix together egg beaters, milk and vanilla. Pour over english muffins. Refrigerate and let soak for at least 8 hours.

Heat greased nonstick skillet over medium heat. When hot, cook muffins, cut-side down, until browned, about 3 minutes. Turn, brown other side, about 3 minutes more.

Serves 6

Cinnamon Caramel Pecan Bread

6 Tbs butter, melted
1/2 cup caramel ice cream topping
1 cup chopped pecans
1 can refrigerated cinnamon rolls (I used Pillsbury regular cinnamon rolls)

Preheat oven to 350.

Combine melted butter, caramel and pecans. Cut each biscuit into 4 pieces and toss in caramel mixture.

Spoon mixture into an 8-inch cake pan. Bake for 20 minutes, or until golden brown. Invert bread onto serving platter and enjoy!

Bubble Up Breakfast Casserole

1 lb sausage, cooked and crumbled
1 can Grands Jr Butter tasting biscuits (10 count)
6 eggs
1 1/4 cup milk
8 oz Velveeta, cubed
1 cup shredded mozzarella
1/4 tsp garlic powder
salt
pepper

Preheat oven to 350 degrees.

Lightly spray a 9x13-inch pan with cooking spray. Quarter biscuits and place in pan. Top with cooked sausage, Velveeta and mozzarella. Whisk together eggs, milk, garlic powder, salt and pepper. Pour over cheese and biscuits.

Bake 30-45 minutes, until golden brown. Allow to cool for 5-10 minutes before serving.
Serves 6

Main Dish

Pollo Loco

Pollo Loco
serves 4

4 boneless, skinless chicken breasts
1 bottle Lawry's Baja Chipotle marinade or Lawry's Mesquite Marinade

3 Tbsp vegetable oil
1 cup uncooked long grain rice (not instant)
1 Tbsp dried minced onion flakes
1 tsp garlic salt
1 tsp Pampered Chef Southwestern Seasoning or Taco Seasoning
2 cups chicken broth
1/2 cup tomato sauce

1 container Mexican Queso (I used Gordo's cheese dip)
chopped tomato

Pour Baja Chipotle Marinade over chicken and let marinate in the refrigerator for 30 minutes or overnight. When ready, grill chicken until done (165 degrees).

While the chicken is grilling prepare the rice.

Heat oil in a large saucepan over medium heat and add rice. Cook, stirring constantly, until puffed and golden. While rice is cooking, sprinkle with salt and Southwestern or Taco Seasoning.

Stir in onion flakes, tomato sauce and chicken broth; bring to a boil. Reduce heat to low, cover and simmer for 20 to 25 minutes. Fluff with a fork.

Heat cheese dip according to package directions set aside.

To assemble the Pollo Loco - place 1/4 of the rice on a plate, top with grilled chicken. Pour 2-3 Tbsp cheese dip over chicken and rice and top with chopped tomatoes.

Crack Burgers

1 1/2 lb ground chuck

3 Tbsp sour cream

2 Tbsp Ranch dressing mix

1/3 cup cooked and crumbled bacon

1 cup shredded cheddar cheese

Combine all ingredients and form into 4 hamburger patties. Grill to desired temperature. The burgers will be very moist, be very careful when you flip them.

Serve on your favorite hamburger bun topped with lettuce, tomato, mustard and mayo.

Serves 4

Italian Pot Roast

1 (3 lb) pot roast (I use a blade roast)
1 Tbsp minced onion
2 Tbsp minced fresh garlic
1 (1 1/4 ounce) package au jus mix
1 (1 ounce) package dried Italian salad dressing mix
2 tsp black pepper
1 pinch cayenne
1 (12-oz) can tomato juice

Place onion and garlic in the bottom of the crock pot, then place the roast on top of them. In a bowl whisk together the tomato juice with both packages of seasonings, black pepper and cayenne. Pour the mixture over the roast.

Cook on low for 8-12 hours or on high for about 4-1/2 hours. Serve over rice or risotto.

Serves 6

Slow Cooker Ham and White Beans

1 lb package dried northern beans
ham bone, hocks, shanks or diced ham (about 1 pound)
2 tsp onion powder
6 cups water
salt & pepper to taste

Rinse and sort the beans for any pebbles. Add the the rinsed beans, onion powder, salt, peppcr, and ham to the crock pot. Add water. Cover and cook on low about 8 hours, until beans are tender. Remove ham bone, shanks or hocks and pull off the meat. Add meat to the crock pot and mix. Serve with cornbread.

Game Day Chili

2 pounds ground chuck
2 Tbsp dried minced onion flakes
4 garlic cloves, minced
2 (15-oz) cans chili beans
3 (8-oz) cans Rotel tomato sauce*
1 (12-oz) bottle beer
1 (14 1/2-oz) can beef broth
1 (6-oz) can tomato paste
2 Tbsp chili powder
1 Tbsp Worcestershire sauce
2 tsp ground cumin
1 tsp ground red pepper
1 tsp paprika
1 tsp hot sauce

Brown meat in a Dutch oven over medium heat, stirring until meat crumbles and is no longer pink. Drain well.

Return meat to Dutch oven. Add garlic and onion flakes. Cook 30 seconds. Add remaining ingredients. Bring to a boil. Reduce heat and simmer 3 hours, or until thickened.

Serves 8

*If you can't find the Ro-tel tomato sauce, use 2 cans of regular tomato sauce and 1 4oz can of green chilies.

Taco Cupcakes

1 lb ground beef
1 packet taco seasoning
2/3 cup water
1 can black beans, drained
2 cups cheddar cheese, shredded
36 wonton wrappers
your favorite taco toppings - salsa, cheese, sour cream, lettuce, tomatoes, etc
cooking spray

Preheat oven to 375.

Brown the meat in a skillet and drain off fat (I use a collander). Return the meat to the skillet; add the taco seasoning, water and black beans. Mix and simmer for 5-10 minutes, until water is absorbed.

Spray 18 regular muffin pan cups with cooking spray. Place one wonton wrapper in each muffin cup. Divide half of the taco meat between muffin cups. Sprinkle half of the cheese over the cupcakes. Repeat layers - wonton, taco meat and cheese.

Bake at 375 for 20 minutes, or until cheese is bubbly. Top with your favorite taco toppings.

Pizza Pot Pie

1 can refrigerated pizza dough
1 jar pizza sauce
18 mozzarella cheese slices (3 per pizza)
pizza toppings - we used sausage, mushrooms & pepperoni
ramekins or oven-safe bowls (my ramekins were 5" x 2.5")
cooking spray

Preheat oven to 425.

Cut 6 circles of dough about one inch larger than ramekin or bowl - you will need to cut 3 circles and re-roll the dough and cut 3 more circles.

Coat the bottom of ramekins or oven-safe bowl with cooking spray. Arrange three mozzarella slices in the bottom and around the sides of the ramekin making sure they overlap. Add mushrooms, sausage and pepperoni (or other fillings) as desired. Ladle the sauce over the fillings just until the ramekin is almost full. Spray the outside of the ramekin with cooking spray, then stretch a round of dough across the top and let hang over the edge.

Bake for 15 minutes until dough is golden. Invert each pizza onto a plate and lift off the ramekin.

Chicken Piccata

Chicken Piccata
serves 4

8 chicken cutlets
2 Tbsp grated Parmesan cheese
1/3 cup flour
Salt and pepper
4 Tbsp olive oil
4 Tbsp butter
1 tsp minced garlic
1 cup chicken broth or dry white wine
6 Tbsp lemon juice
dash red pepper flakes
1/4 cup brined capers, rinsed

Mix together the flour, salt, pepper, and grated Parmesan. Rinse the chicken pieces in water. Dredge them thoroughly in the flour mixture, until well coated.

Heat olive oil and 2 tablespoons of the butter in a large skillet on medium high heat. Add half of the chicken pieces. Brown well on each side, about 3 minutes per side. Remove the chicken from the pan and reserve to a plate. Cook the other breasts in the same manner, remove from pan. Cover with aluminum foil and keep warm in the oven while you prepare the sauce.

Add the chicken broth or white wine, lemon juice, red pepper, and capers to the pan. Scrape up the browned bits. Continue cooking until the sauce is reduced by half. Plate the chicken and serve with the sauce poured over the chicken. Serve over angel hair pasta, if desired.

Rosemary Ranch Chicken

1/2 cup olive oil
1/2 cup ranch dressing
3 Tbsp Worcestershire sauce
1 Tbsp dried rosemary
1 tsp salt
1 tsp lemon juice
1 tsp white vinegar
1/4 tsp ground black pepper
1 Tbsp white sugar
4 skinless, boneless chicken breast halves, pounded to an even thickness

In a medium bowl, stir together the olive oil, ranch dressing, Worcestershire sauce, rosemary, salt, lemon juice, white vinegar, pepper, and sugar.

Place chicken in the gallon size ziplock bag, and stir to coat with the marinade. Cover and refrigerate for at least 8 hours (all day).

Preheat the grill for medium-high heat. Grill chicken for 8 to 12 minutes, or until the chicken is no longer pink in the center, and the juices run clear.

Bread and Side Dishes

Skillet Corn

3 cups corn kernels (I use frozen)
1/2 tsp salt
1/4 tsp pepper
1 Tbsp sugar
1/4 cup butter
1/2 cup water
1 Tbsp flour
1/4 cup milk

In a large skillet, combine corn, salt, pepper, sugar, butter and water. Cover and simmer 15 minutes on medium heat, stirring occasionally.

Combine flour with milk, blending until smooth. Stir into corn. Cook five more minutes, stirring constantly.

Muffin Tin Potato Gratin

2 medium russet potatoes (about 3/4 pound each)
dried rosemary
salt
pepper
6 Tbsp heavy cream

Preheat oven to 400.

Spray 6 standard muffin cups with cooking spray. Thinly slice potatoes. Place 2 slices in each up and season with coarse salt, ground pepper and rosemary.

Continue adding potatoes, seasoning every two slices, until cups are filled. Pour 1 tablespoon heavy cream over each.

Bake until potatoes are golden brown and tender when pierced with a knife, 30-35 minutes. Run a thin knife around each gratin. Place a baking sheet or large plate over pan and invert to release gratins. Flip right side up and serve.

Gnocchi Mac and Cheese

Gnocchi Mac and Cheese

1 pound gnocchi
2 Tbsp butter
2 tsp minced garlic
1 Tbsp all-purpose flour
3/4 cup milk
1 tsp Dijon mustard
1/4 cup shredded Gruyere cheese
1/4 cup shredded fontina cheese
1 tsp basil
Salt and pepper to taste
1/3 cup shredded Parmigiano-Reggiano

Preheat oven to 375.

Prepare gnocchi according to package directions. Drain and place gnocchi in a single-layer in a 1-1/2 quart shallow baking dish that has been sprayed with nonstick spray.

Melt butter in a medium saucepan over medium heat. Stir in garlic and cook until fragrant, about 30 seconds. Whisk in flour until it thickens and bubbles, then whisk in milk and Dijon. Continue to whisk mixture and cook until slightly thickened, about 3-5 minutes.

Combine Gruyere and fontina, then add by the handful to milk mixture, stirring until melted before adding the next handful. Once all cheese is melted, add basil, salt and pepper.

Pour sauce over gnocchi and sprinkle with Parmigiano-Reggiano over top. Bake gnocchi until they puff and cheese is golden and bubbly, about 25 minutes. Let gnocchi rest for 5 minutes before serving.

Ranch Green Beans

28 oz can green beans, drained
1/2 cup chicken broth
1 packet ranch dressing mix
1/4 cup bacon pieces

Combine all ingredients in a large sauce pan. Heat over medium heat for 10 minutes.
Serves 8

Crack Potatoes

2 (16oz) containers sour cream
2 cups cheddar cheese, shredded
2 (3oz) bags real bacon bits
2 packages Ranch Dip mix
1 large (32 oz) bag frozen shredded hash brown potatoes
2 cups cornflakes, crushed
1/4 cup butter, cubed

Preheat oven to 400.

Combine first 4 ingredients, mix in hash browns. Spread into a 9x13 pan. Top with crushed cornflakes and cubed butter.

Bake 45-60 minutes.
Serves 10

I divided the potato mixture into 3 small 7x7 disposable foil pans and froze them. I wrapped them with plastic wrap and then foil. Just add a few minutes to the baking time if baking from frozen.

Steakhouse Sauteed Mushrooms

3 Tbsp butter
1 pound fresh mushrooms, sliced (I used a mixture of white, baby bella and shiitake)
1 Tbsp dried minced onion
1/4 cup dry white wine
1/4 tsp salt
1/4 tsp pepper
1 clove garlic, pressed
2 tsp Worcestershire sauce

Melt butter in large skillet. Add mushrooms and sauté for a few minutes, until mushrooms start to soften. Stir in remaining ingredients and cook uncovered over low heat for 30 minutes or until mushrooms are tender.

Serves 4

Bacon Mac and Cheese with Gruyere

4 cups heavy cream
4 Tbsp fresh rosemary, chopped (or 4 tsp dried rosemary)
Salt and cracked black pepper to taste
1/2 pound bacon, diced, fried crisp and drained
1 pound elbow macaroni
2 cups (8 ounces) Gruyère cheese, grated

Cook pasta according to package directions and drain, reserving 1 tablespoon pasta water.

Place cream in large saucepan with rosemary. Add salt and pepper. Bring to boil and keep at boil until reduced by half.

Stir in bacon and pasta and simmer until hot; add the Gruyère cheese and 1 tablespoon of pasta water. Stir until cheese is melted. Serve immediately.
Serves 6

Butter Dips

1/4 cup unsalted butter
1 1/4 cup flour
2 tsp sugar
2 tsp baking powder
1 tsp kosher salt
2/3 - 1 cup buttermilk

Heat the oven to 450°F. Cut the butter into pieces and place them in a 8-inch square microwave safe baking dish. Put the dish in the microwave and melt the butter. You can also put the baking dish in the oven to melt the butter as it pre-heats. (The dish in the microwave is just faster.)

While the butter is melting, whisk the flour, sugar, baking powder, and salt together in a large mixing bowl. Stir in 2/3 cup buttermilk; continue to add more buttermilk until a loose dough forms. (I used about 2-3 Tbsp more than the 2/3 cup)

Remove baking dish from the microwave/oven and press biscuit dough in the pan over the melted butter (It helps to put a little flour on top of the dough or your fingers). Using a knife, cut the biscuits into 12 squares. Bake for 12-15 minutes until golden.

7 UP Biscuits

2 cups Bisquick
1/2 cup sour cream
1/2 cup 7-up
1/4 cup melted butter

Preheat oven to 450.

Stir together sour cream into biscuit mix. Add 7-Up, stir until just combined. This dough will be very soft.

Sprinkle additional biscuit mix on board or table and pat dough out. (You may need to add a little more Bisquick to get to the top of the dough.)

Melt 1/4 cup butter in a 9 inch square pan. Cut 9 biscuits out of dough.

Place cut biscuits in pan and bake for 12-15 minutes or until golden brown.

Makes 9 biscuits

Cheesy Biscuits

1 1/2 cups Bisquick
3/4 cup buttermilk
3 Tbsp sugar
1/4 tsp vanilla
1 cup cheddar cheese, shredded

Preheat oven to 425.

Stir together all ingredients just until combined. Scoop into a mini muffin pan coated with cooking spray. Bake 12-15 minutes, until golden.

Makes 20 biscuits

Tailgating

Cheddar Bacon Ranch Pulls

1 unsliced loaf of (round is preferable) sourdough bread
8-12 oz cheddar cheese, thinly sliced
3 oz bag Oscar Mayer Real Bacon bits
1/2 cup butter, melted
1 Tbsp Ranch dressing mix

Using a sharp bread knife cut the bread going both directions. Do not cut through the bottom crust. Place slices of cheese in between cuts. Sprinkle bacon bits on bread, making sure to get in between cuts. Mix together butter and Ranch dressing mix. Pour over bread. Wrap in foil the entire loaf in foil and place on a baking sheet.

Bake at 350 degrees for 15 minutes. Unwrap. Bake for an additional 10 minutes, or until cheese is melted.

Cream Cheese Sausage Balls

1 lb hot sausage, uncooked
8 oz cream cheese, softened
1 1/4 cups Bisquick
4 oz cheddar cheese, shredded

Preheat oven to 400F.

Mix all ingredients until well combined. (I use my KitchenAid mixer with the dough hook attachment) Roll into 1-inch balls. Bake for 20-25 minutes, or until brown.

Sausage balls may be frozen uncooked. If baking frozen, add a few minutes to the baking time.

Sausage Biscuit Bites

2 (10 count) cans flaky biscuits (Grands Jr)
1 lb sausage (Tennessee Pride)
2 cups shredded cheddar cheese

Preheat oven to 400.

Mix uncooked sausage and cheese gently until well blended. Shape into 40 balls of equal size.

Remove biscuits from cans and separate each biscuit into two layers, making 40 total biscuit layers. Press one layer of biscuit into cup of lightly greased mini-cupcake pan. Repeat with remaining layers.

Place sausage-cheese ball in each biscuit cup. Bake for 8 to 10 minutes or until biscuits are browned and sausage balls are bubbly.

Sausage and Pepperoni Pizza Puffs

3/4 cup flour
3/4 tsp baking powder
1/2 tsp garlic powder
3/4 cup whole milk
1 egg, lightly beaten
4 oz mozzarella cheese, shredded (about 1 cup)
2 oz mini turkey pepperoni, (about 1/2 cup)
4 oz low-fat sausage, cooked and crumbled
1/2 cup pizza sauce

Pre-heat the oven to 375.

Grease a 24-cup mini-muffin pan. In a large bowl, whisk together the flour, garlic powder and baking powder; whisk in the milk and egg. Stir in the mozzarella, sausage and pepperoni; let stand for 10 minutes.

Stir the batter and divide among the mini-muffin cups. Bake until puffed and golden, 20 to 25 minutes.

Meanwhile, microwave the pizza sauce until warmed through. Serve the puffs with the pizza sauce for dipping.

Mississippi Sin Dip

Mississippi Sin Dip

16oz sour cream

8oz cream cheese, softened

2 cup cheddar cheese, shredded

1/2 cup chopped ham

1 green onion, chopped

1/4 tsp hot sauce

1 tsp Worcestershire sauce

salt

pepper

16 oz French bread loaf

In a mixing bowl, combine all ingredients, except French bread; stirring until well blended.

Cut a thin slice from top of bread loaf; set slice aside. Using a gentle sawing motion, cut vertically to, but not through, bottom of the loaf, 1/2 inch from the edge, to cut out center of bread. Lift out center of loaf. Fill hollowed bread loaf with the dip. Wrap loaf with foil.

Bake dip at 350° degrees for 1 hour. Serve with reserved bread cubes, crackers, or potato chips.

BBQ Chicken Dip

12 oz cooked chicken, chopped
1 (8oz) block cream cheese, softened
3/4 cup BBQ sauce
1/4 cup ranch dressing
1/4 cup sour cream
1 1/2 cup cheddar cheese, shredded
1 green onion, chopped

Preheat oven to 350.

In a mixing bowl combine chicken, cream cheese, sour cream, ranch dressing, barbecue sauce, and 1 cup of cheddar cheese. Pour mixture into a lightly greased 8x8 baking dish. Top the dip with chopped green onion and remaining cheese. Bake for 25-30 minutes or until bubbly.

Baked Buffalo Wings

4 pounds chicken drumettes
2 cups Frank's hot sauce, divided
½ cup butter
Bleu cheese dressing
Ranch dressing
Celery sticks

Put chicken pieces in a plastic bag. Pour 1 cup of hot sauce over wing and toss to coat. Seal bag and let marinate for a few hours or overnight in the refrigerator.

Preheat oven to 400°.

Line a baking sheet with foil and set rack inside. Place chicken pieces on rack and discard marinade. Bake for 30 minutes. Flip wings and cook 15-20 minutes longer, until chicken is crispy.

Meanwhile, combine butter and hot sauce in small saucepan and cook over medium heat, whisking until combined. Transfer wings to large bowl, add sauce, toss to thoroughly coat, and serve immediately with blue cheese or ranch dressing and celery sticks.

Club Sandwich Puffs

1 oz deli ham, chopped
1 oz deli turkey, chopped
1 oz deli roast beef, chopped
2 slices bacon, cooked and chopped
1 tsp onion powder
1/2 cup cheddar cheese, shredded
1 egg
1 Tbsp honey mustard dressing
1 (8 ounce) package refrigerated crescent dinner rolls

Preheat oven to 350 degrees.

In a small bowl combine finely chopped ham, turkey, roast beef, bacon, onion powder, cheese, egg, and mustard. Mix well.

Lightly spray a mini muffin pan with non stick cooking spray.

Unroll crescent rolls and press dough into one large rectangle. Cut rectangle into 24 squares. Press dough squares into muffin cups and shape up around the edges.

Fill each muffin cup with some of the meat mixture. Bake 13-15 minutes or until lightly browned.

Mozzarella Cheese Ball

8 oz package cream cheese, softened
1/2 package (4 1/2 tsp) dry ranch dressing mix
1/3 cup mayonnaise
2 cup shredded mozzarella cheese
finely chopped pecans

Combine first 4 ingredients in a bowl. Mix well.
Form mixture into a ball and roll in chopped pecans.
Refrigerate before serving with crackers.

Football Twinkie Pops

Twinkies
6-inch cookie sticks
Chocolate Almond Bark or Chocolate Candy Melts

Icing
2 cups powdered sugar
3 Tbsp light corn syrup
1-2 Tbsp milk
1/2 tsp almond extract

Unwrap Twinkies. Melt chocolate according to package directions. Dip cookie stick 1/3 of the way into the melted chocolate. Push stick into center of the end of the Twinkie. Place on a wax paper lined cookie sheet. Repeat with remaining Twinkies. Freeze for 15 minutes.

Dip the twinkies into melted chocolate, coating fully. Shake off excess and place on wax paper lined cookie sheet. Repeat with remaining Twinkies. Freeze for 10 minutes.

Prepare icing. Mix together powdered sugar, corn syrup, almond extract and 1 Tbsp of milk. Add more milk if needed. You want the icing thick enough to pipe on the Twinkies. Fill a piping bag with icing and use tip #3 to pipe football laces and tip #104 to pipe stripes. Allow icing to set before serving.

Dessert

Peanut Butter Eclair Cake

1 box chocolate graham crackers (there will be a few graham crackers left over)
2 (3 1/4-ounce) boxes vanilla instant pudding
1 cup peanut butter
3 1/2 cups milk
1 (8-ounce) container Cool Whip, thawed
1 can chocolate frosting

Spray the bottom of a 9x13 pan with cooking spray. Line the bottom of the pan with whole graham crackers. In bowl of an electric mixer, mix pudding with milk and peanut butter; beat at medium speed for 2 minutes. Fold in whipped topping. Pour half the pudding mixture over graham crackers. Place another layer of whole graham crackers on top of pudding layer. Pour over remaining half of pudding mixture and cover with another layer of graham crackers.

Heat the container of prepared frosting, uncovered in the microwave for 1 minute. Pour over the top of the cake. Refrigerate for at least 12 hours before serving.

Serves 12

Krispy Kreme Ice Cream

3/4 cup sugar
2 tablespoons cornstarch
1/8 teaspoon salt
2 cups milk
1 cup heavy whipping cream
1 egg yolk
1 1/2 teaspoons vanilla bean paste or vanilla extract
5 Krispy Kreme glazed doughnuts

Whisk together first 3 ingredients in a large heavy saucepan. Gradually whisk in milk and cream. Cook over medium heat, stirring constantly, 10 to 12 minutes or until mixture thickens slightly. Remove from heat. Whisk egg yolk until slightly thickened.

Gradually whisk about 1 cup hot cream mixture into yolk. Add yolk mixture to remaining cream mixture, whisking constantly. Whisk in vanilla bean paste. Cool 1 hour, stirring occasionally. Place plastic wrap directly on cream mixture, and chill 8 to 24 hours.

Chop Krispy Kreme doughnuts into small pieces. Stir 1/4 of the chopped doughnuts into the cream mixture. Pour mixture into freezer container of a 1 1/2-qt. electric ice-cream maker, and freeze according to manufacturer's instructions. Once the ice cream is set, stir in remaining Krispy Kreme doughnuts and put in freezer to harden.

Butterfinger Cupcakes

Butterfinger Cupcakes
24 cupcakes

1 box Devil's Food Cake mix, plus ingredients to make cake
1 can fudge frosting

4 cups chocolate chips
6 Tbsp canola oil

3 (3.7 oz) King Size Butterfingers

Quick Buttercream Frosting
18 Tbsp butter, softened
6 Tbsp milk
1 Tbsp vanilla
6 3/4 cups powdered sugar

Prepare cupcakes according to directions on cake mix package. Let cupcakes cool completely.

Using a sharp knife, cut a circle out on top of the cupcake. Make your cut go about halfway into the cupcake. Remove the cake chunk and fill the hole will fudge frosting (I used two spoons to scoop the frosting into the hole). Invert the cupcake chunk on top of the fudge frosting - you want the extra cake to be sticking up.

Prepare the buttercream frosting. Mix together all the ingredients and beat on medium for 3 minutes, until fluffy. Transfer frosting into a piping bag and pipe frosting on top of the cupcakes, covering the cake chunk. Let the frosting set up for 30 minutes.

While the frosting is setting up, crush the Butterfingers in the food processor until completely pulverized. **I froze the Butterfingers and crushed them frozen.**

Combine chocolate chips and oil in a medium microwave-safe bowl. Heat on HIGH for 1 minute. Stir and continue to heat at 30 second intervals until completely melted. Allow to cool for 5-10 minutes before using. (You might want to do this in two batches so the chocolate doesn't harden while you dip the cupcakes) Dip the frosted cupcakes into the chocolate - I used a spoon to hold the frosting into place to make sure it didn't fall off the cupcake. Immediately coat the cupcake with the pulverized Butterfingers - just smash it all over the chocolate. Repeat until all cupcakes are dipped and covered. Refrigerate approximately 1 hour to allow the chocolate to set up.

Almond Toffee Bars

1 1/2 cups rolled oats
1/2 cup graham cracker crumbs
1/4 tsp fine salt
1/2 cup unsalted butter, melted
1 cup skor toffee bits (I used one bag of regular Heath Toffee Bits)
1 cup chocolate chips
1 cup sliced almonds
1 can (300 ml) sweetened condensed milk

Preheat the oven to 350F. Grease and line an 8-inch square pan with parchment paper so that the paper hangs over the sides of the pan.

Stir the oats, graham cracker crumbs and salt in a bowl to combine, then stir in the melted butter. Pres the crumbly oat mixture into the bottom of the prepared pan. Sprinkle skor bits evenly on top, followed by chocolate chips and sliced almonds.

Pour the sweetened condensed milk evenly over pan (it will sink in as it bakes) and bake for 30-40 minutes, or until the top is golden brown and the edges are bubbling. Cool to room temperature in the pan, then chill for at least 4 hours before slicing into bars.

Store toffee bars in the refrigerator for up to one week. Makes about 25 squares.

Nutella Gooey Butter Cake

Cake:
1 (18 1/4-ounce) package devil's food cake mix
1 egg
8 tablespoons butter, melted

Filling:
1 (8-ounce) package cream cheese, softened
1 cup Nutella
3 eggs
1 teaspoon vanilla
8 tablespoons butter, melted
1 (16-ounce) box powdered sugar

Preheat oven to 350.

Combine the cake mix, egg, and butter and mix well with an electric mixer. Pat the mixture into the bottom of a lightly greased 13 by 9-inch baking pan.

To make the filling: In a large bowl, beat the cream cheese and Nutella until smooth. Add the eggs, vanilla, and butter, and beat together. Next, add the powdered sugar and mix well. Spread Nutella mixture over cake batter and bake for 40 to 50 minutes. Make sure not to overbake as the center should be a little gooey.

Serve with fresh whipped cream.

Lemon Velvet Cream Pie

Lemon Velvet Cream Pie

Crust
1 1/2 c graham cracker crumbs
5 Tbsp sugar
1/3 c butter, melted

Filling
1 tsp. unflavored gelatin
2 Tbsp cold water
6 egg yolks
1 1/2 14-oz. cans sweetened condensed milk (2 cups)
1/4 cup whipping cream
1/4 tsp. salt
3/4 cup lemon juice

Topping
1 c heavy whipping cream
1/4 c powdered sugar
1 tsp vanilla

Preheat oven to 375 degrees F.

Crust: Combine all ingredients and press against sides and bottom of springform pan. (I use a measuring cup to do this - works great!) Set aside.

In a small bowl soften gelatin in water 5 minutes. Heat in microwave for 14 seconds; set aside.

In large bowl combine egg yolks and sweetened condensed milk. With an electric mixer, beat on high speed for 2 to 3 minutes until well combined. Beat in gelatin, whipping cream and salt on low speed. Add lemon juice and beat on low speed for 30 seconds. Pour into prepared crust.

Bake 22 to 25 minutes or until center of pie looks set when gently shaken; cool on wire rack 1 hour. Cover loosely and refrigerate at least 2 hours.

Topping: Place the heavy cream in a chilled mixing bowl. Whip until the whisk begins to leave tracks in the bowl. Add the sugar and vanilla and whip until the cream holds a medium peak. Spread on top of pie.

Pumpkin Crunch

1 15oz can pumpkin
1 12-oz can evaporated milk
1 cup sugar
1 tsp pumpkin spice
3 eggs
1 18.25 oz box yellow cake mix
1 cup chopped pecans
3/4 cup butter, cut in pieces
1 12oz container cool-whip
8 oz cream cheese, softened
1/2 cup confectioners sugar

Preheat oven to 350.

Mix pumpkin, milk, sugar, pumpkin spice and eggs and pour into 9x13 baking dish. Sprinkle cake mix on top. Sprinkle pecans on top of cake mix. Cover nuts with pieces of butter.

Bake for one hour. Let cool completely. Beat cool-whip, cream cheese and confectioners sugar together and spread on top.

Homemade Butterfingers

1 lb. candy corn
16oz jar peanut butter (I used Peter Pan Honey Roasted peanut butter)
16oz pkg. chocolate candy coating

Melt candy corn in microwave on high 1 minute. Stir and continue cooking in 15-second intervals until melted, stirring after each interval. Stir in peanut butter.

Spread mixture in an 8x8 pan lined with parchment. Cool completely.

Cut into squares. Dip in melted chocolate candy coating. Lay on waxed paper to set.

Peppermint Cookies and Cream Popcorn Bark

2 bags microwave popcorn, popped
1 (6oz) box candy canes, crushed
1 package Oreo cookies, crushed
1 1/2 (24oz) packs Almond Bark
1 1/2 tsp peppermint extract or a few drops of peppermint oil

Place popcorn in a very large bowl - the biggest one you have. Pour crushed candy canes and Oreos on top of the popcorn. (I crush my candy canes and Oreos in the food processor) Melt one pack of almond bark according to instructions on the package. Add the peppermint extract or oil to the almond bark and pour over popcorn. Stir. The Oreos will absorb some of the almond bark and the popcorn won't be fully coated. Melt the remaining almond bark and pour over popcorn. Stir until popcorn is coated. Pour popcorn on wax paper and allow to harden. Once the popcorn has hardened, break into pieces and enjoy!

Microwave Peanut Brittle

1 cup sugar
1/2 cup light corn syrup (Karo)
1 Tbsp butter
1 tsp vanilla
1 cup peanuts (I use lightly salted cocktail peanuts)
1 tsp baking soda

Combine sugar and syrup in a microwave safe bowl (I use a glass bowl), stir. Microwave on high for 5 minutes. Add butter, vanilla and peanuts; stir. Microwave on high for 1 minute 30 seconds.

Remove bowl from microwave and quickly stir in baking soda. Immediately pour mixture onto parchment paper, aluminum foil or a Silpat.

Spread into a rectangle and let cool for 1 hour. Break into pieces and enjoy!

ABOUT THE AUTHOR

Stephanie Parker is a full-time Accounting Manager and author of the *Plain Chicken* food blog. She also writes a weekly food column in *The Birmingham News* and a popular blog on www.al.com.

Stephanie's recipes have been featured on the Rhodes Bread blog, TODAY show Food Blog, The New York Times blog, Wisconsin Cheese Talk blog and Our Own Labels blog. In 2011, she won the TODAY Home Chef Challenge contest, and her recipe is in the TODAY Show recipe database. She has also been featured in *The Birmingham Magazine* and in the January 2013 *Southern Living Magazine*.

Stephanie lives in Birmingham, AL with her husband and three cats.

www.plainchicken.com
facebook.com/plainchicken.fan
pinterest.com/plainchicken
instagram.com/plainchicken

Stephanie Parker

24778856R00039

Made in the USA
Lexington, KY
31 July 2013